Simple .

Brenda Eldridge

Simple Pleasures

Simple Pleasures
ISBN 978 1 76109 678 5
Copyright © text Brenda Eldridge 2024
Cover image: Libertad from Pixabay

First published 2024 by
GINNINDERRA PRESS
PO Box 3461 Port Adelaide 5015
www.ginninderrapress.com.au

Contents

Dancing on Air

Silver gull soaring sweeping
above the waterline
not keeping me company
as I first thought

He had another partner
to celebrate the morning with
a welcome swallow darting
in perfect unison
together they were dancing on air

Green Goddess Lily

She takes my breath away each time I see her
feet in a trickling stream on a mountainside
surrounded by lush leaves – tropical and vivid

Her trumpet flower impossibly green
white centre merely highlighting her mystery
making me want to reach for a paintbrush
to bring her to my idea of completeness
such is my arrogance
as if I could improve on the exquisite

Up on the Roof

For over half a century
magpies warbling have thrilled my senses
they are for me the sound of Australia

I heard a pair exchanging opinions
but could not see them
I stepped from my studio onto the balcony
looked up and there they were
not elegant on a fencepost but
rather windswept standing on the roof
one with beak pointed straight up
as if singing to the small patch of
blue sky among sun-filled clouds

Ibis

To see them wading in muddy shallows
great curved beaks
stabbing the soft ooze for food
it is hard to imagine them in flight
those same beaks thrusting forward
wings all harnessed power and strength
then coming down to land
as graceful as any ballerina
a gentle feathering action
to sink to the stage below

Snails

To my disgust a watermelon tasted terrible
so I donated the remaining half
to the birds in the garden

Bob the wattlebird showed his disdain
and ignored its rosy soft flesh
which surprised me as I have seen
how he licks the mango stones clean

Snails have a different notion of discerning taste –
a dozen or more were clinging to the rim
and over a few days devoured the contents
leaving an empty shell

Saved

Rain falling makes no noise
until it lands on something
then the air is filled with the pattering
of water drops on a billion leaves
softly thudding on mulch and path
drumming on roof tiles
splashing in a bird bath

Parched earth makes no noise
as it soaks up drops of moisture
it softens   becomes plump
sighs with relief
and settles

Roots like threads of silk
drink deeply
flowers brighten
vegetables fatten with flavour
and we are saved from extinction
for a bit longer

Spring Gifts

Sun warm on my face
a flicker of a breeze
ocean lapping around my ankles
a bigger wave washing my calves
smooth   sensuous
these are the gifts of this
late spring morning

Choosing Your Fights

Tiny willy-wagtail
making dive-bomb attacks
on a magpie strutting by
looking for breakfast

Size doesn't matter
it's the strength of spirit
coupled with the wisdom
to choose your fights

Tropical Breakfast

A pair of New Holland honeyeaters
are darting about the riverside garden

They pause mid-flight
to cling to the orange tropicana lily
sipping nectar for breakfast

while the sparrows look
for scattered breadcrumbs
I haven't put out yet

Borage

Was ever a sky so blue above
an apothecary's garden
where borage grows
slender arched stems
covered in a fuzz of soft silvery spikes
delicate bloom hanging from each stem
petals like insect wings
poised ready to take flight
so pretty nestled on my lavender panna cotta

Held in Balance

A sparrowhawk hovered lazily
on the early morning air
I've not seen one so close to home before

There was a tension about it that said
it would be ready to dive
with a flick of wing tips
when those sharp eyes saw movement below

Scrubby bushes   dried grasses
ideal hiding places for small creatures
but they must move eventually
searching for food or taking it to babies nearby

It was a waiting game
life or death held in balance by patience

Sunshine and Shadow

No matter how heavy my heart
my spirit is lifted by the play of
sunlight and dancing leaves flickering endlessly
or watching the careless passing of clouds
with their dark centres and gleaming edges
creating patches of blue

A cloudless sky is almost
too much of a good thing
the shadows remind me
nothing remains the same for long
not the good or the bad
but without the sun we would not be

Moon and Venus

In the unique clarity of a pre-dawn sky
it was a golden sickle moon
escorted by Venus
who brought a prayer of thanksgiving
and a smile to my lips

For my poem
I thought to do research about
names given to this celestial pair
and decided Shakespeare had it right –
'a rose by any other name would smell as sweet…'

Hawaiian Surfrider Hibiscus

A name which conjures up
tropical beaches and palm trees –
five petals slightly crumpled
as if folded too long in a traveller's suitcase
glowing like warm sunshine
heart a simple crimson flower shape
of rounded petals like a child might draw
central stamen like a honey drizzler
both erotic and exotic

Blackbird

Blackbirds stopped singing near our garden
and I missed their golden notes
lingering on the morning air

But Mother Nature has worked her magic
and seeing bark scuffed along the path edges
and hearing a sudden alarmed call
I knew they had returned

As we sat in the garden for lunch
I was delighted to see a young one
feathers still more brown than black
scurrying among the bushes
looking for crumbs we had tossed aside
and not troubled at all by our presence

It was perfectly at home in our haven

Layer Upon Layer

Living on the flat plain
close to tidal reach and ocean
I sometimes forget
the climb up into the hills
road winding through tree-lined streets
with large gracious houses
through a tunnel blasted in the mountain
and beyond the crest of the hills
a view to make me pause

Surrounded by tall gum trees
I look across a valley clothed
in the vibrant colours of autumn
knowing somewhere there is a hidden lake
and beyond layer upon layer
of blue-grey hills sleeping
beneath a pale blue sky

Grey Morning

A grey morning does not mean
my spirits must be overcast
I can see the tidal reach
as a sheet of beaten pewter
still wonder what creatures are
hidden beneath the surface
smile at streetlights with distorted reflections

Sun shining on leaves
sparkling with raindrops
is not the only way to have
a good start to the day

Thunder and Lightning

As children we used to count the seconds
between a flash of lightning
and the crash of thunder
the gap between getting less
as the storm came closer

There was something ordered and predictable
as if the storm knew it could not pass by
until all the windows had been rattled
the garden drenched in a downpour…
then it could rumble and grumble away
into the distance

It isn't the same living here by the sea in Australia
I watch fabulous displays of sheet lightning
flickering and dancing across the heavens
gasp at the vicious forks striking land and water
but I haven't been able to neatly count seconds
between lightning and thunder
I can't tell how quickly a storm is approaching
there have been times
when with no warning
a single clap of thunder is overhead
threatening to squash the house
with the weight of its ferocity

I walk along a beach carefully looking
out across the gulf at flashes of lightning
thinking that my cycle tyres are rubber
and if I get struck I am unlikely to be fried
and my dad's words echoing from long ago
not to shelter under a tree –
which is silly as there are none on the beach…
such are my scurrying thoughts
as I plod as quickly as I can
cycle cumbersome in soft sand
the relief of a solid path
pedalling like mad to get home safe

Pondering in the ocean

First hot morning of spring
a promise of summer coming soon
wading into the luxurious cold ocean
swimming under water
entering another world
where sound is different
and I become weightless
as my arms and legs propel me along
I am no mermaid
and must come up for air

Rolling over and floating
drifting like a starfish
feeling a magical embrace…
being held by firmness
or nothing
I don't know which

I watch the blue sky
think about the vastness that is tangible
and measurable if we only knew how

I think about thoughts and emotions
my spirit   my soul
they are intangible
immeasurable
which means they have no limits
and I am free to love whoever and however I want

Abandoned Wheelbarrow

Why does an old wheelbarrow
on a building site evoke such nostalgia?

In these days of mechanical equipment
it was a surprise to even see one
obviously being used for a while
then left as if at the end of a shift
or rain stopped play
but still there unmoved days later

I scrambled among mud and weeds
to take photographs for old times sake
and was transported back sixty years
to the days when a wheelbarrow
was commonplace in the village
and on the farm
not that they were ever left out carelessly
rather dirt and detritus hosed off
and wheeled into a shed or barn…

Buttered Toast

Darkened room of late afternoon
open fireplace
coals glowing red   orange
hot on my face
as I sit on the rug
close enough to the fire
to toast my piece of bread

Not an evenly sliced piece
our baker delivered whole loaves
and it depended on how sharp
the blade of the bread knife
how thin the slices were

Mine were usually thin on one side
getting thicker towards the other
which made sticking it
to the toasting fork
a rather haphazard affair
and my toast was often
lightly brown or almost black

I didn't mind because
once the butter was on
I was in some kind of heaven

Tapestry

With one stitch at a time
I create a house
a boat
a lake
a mountain

Like my life
one stitch at a time
I create
a beautiful tapestry
of dark and light threads
harmonising

Flags

Orange and yellow petals of a tropicana lily
are flickering and dancing in a blustery wind
making me think of flags flying
reminding me of all the pomp and circumstance
associated with these emblems of a nations identity

Some people take inordinate pride watching a flag flying
seeing it as a sign of possession –
like the one left up on the moon by arrogant Americans
who also left their rubbish there for posterity

Hearts stir seeing a flag flying on a castle tower
showing that royalty are in residence
or at half-mast declaring the death of someone significant

They are used to direct traffic
signal messages in semaphore
and capitulation in a war in days of old

I think I prefer the flags that are irises
growing on the banks of a river
their sunny yellow faces
gifting passers-by a moment of joy and delight

My Spirit May Soar

I dare myself to
look up into the vast heavens
read about the universe
and dream

My spirit may soar
on wings of music or
colours in clouds at dawn or sunset
birds in flight
or a newborn baby's cry

I might wish to jump from a plane
swim like a dolphin
kayak on our tidal reach before breakfast…
but I have feet of clay
and a love of earth between my fingers
as I plant flowers to adorn our garden
and provide nectar for the birds

Coming to the Rescue

A visitor was in the empty bath –
not a spider – a lizard
as short as my little finger
suctioned toes unable
to get purchase
to climb sheer walls
and away to freedom

He only needed some help
from a carefully placed glass
and a sheet of paper
the intrepid hunter not me
but my gentle man
coming to the rescue
of us all

An easing of hard reality

Blue-green Australian trees
rich green tree ferns

Like tall flames
slender poplars and maples
shone lemon yellow
mellow gold
vivid russets
bright crimson
deep maroon
all laced with sunlight

Tiny wrens
mother and joey kangaroo
mocking kookaburra
melodious magpie

A day of easing hard reality
not changing it
making it a little easier to bear

Solitude

For ten years I lived alone
before he came into my life

He understood from the beginning
even as we built a life together
I needed times of solitude

And so three times a week after breakfast
regardless of rain or shine
I go off on my bicycle
reciting before I leave his office the ritual:
Watch out for the silly bastards on the road
Use my gears and brakes properly
Flash nicely (lights – not revealing what
is beneath my coat)
Enjoy myself
COME HOME SAFE

I tootle along mindful of the ritual words
looking at flowers   trees   birds
down to the beach
where I walk along the waterline
pushing my bike in the wet sand –
yes it does cause rust
but that is small price
for this time to empty my head and heart
of the cares of a life well lived
and silence to pray for strength and support

I head for home knowing he is waiting
not relaxing until I am inside the garden gate
and he hears the click as it locks
then listening patiently to me burble
about progress of building sites
issues with dogs and their owners
just the ordinary things
that make this life so rich

Temptation

Walking along a city street in the early morning
when the busy world is just waking up
and the unmistakable smell of bacon cooking
wafts across your senses
and even though you aren't hungry at all
the idea of a bacon sandwich dripping
with melted butter and tomato sauce
is sooo compelling
accompanied of course by
the irresistible smell of freshly perked coffee...

Coffee in the Mall

Requesting a coffee I didn't really want
while waiting for my bike to be serviced
I made a fun connection
with the woman taking orders in the cafe

She was new on the job
not so much young just nervous

We joked about how many different kinds
of coffee there are these days
and our own tastes being very simple

A bored-sounding white youth
helped her with the computer
his attitude doing nothing to lift her angst

I smiled with her –
her inherent politeness
clearly part of her colourful heritage

Continuity

They sat together weaving more than baskets
gentle laughter a universal language
agile fingers making something complex seem easy

Complex yes but not complicated by
hidden ugly agendas or
nuances of going-one-better

Some women were the natural teachers
others willing learners
but they all had something valuable to contribute

Beneath them soft green grass
courtesy of wasteful watering
but oh how wonderful it felt

Tall trees towered around them
not all native to this area
but no one could deny their calming presence

Birds pecking dropped lunch crumbs
being tempted away from what is good for them
making them like us –
sometimes preferring a more easeful way

Something within all yearned for long ago days
a different pace   different values

Sometimes none of us know how to go forward
except perhaps with more days spent
weaving baskets in a park
reminding ourselves   at heart   we are all the same

Holding Hands

A simple thing to hold hands
coming with many hidden messages

We do it to keep a small child close by and safe
or a naughty one to restrict their waywardness
as we navigate the supermarket aisles
with their tempting displays

We hold hands with a new love
a statement of togetherness
a declaration of caring
almost a warning of 'this one is with me'

We hold a beloved by the hand
to forge a link we hope will last and last

If we are already mature
we smile as other people smile to see
two oldies walking hand in hand

Yes it is a simple thing
that brings comfort
a feeling of belonging
or perhaps I waited so long before I had this
I place more value on it than others might

Heartwarming

In the supermarket
I couldn't help noticing
a young man and his daughter –
but not just for their exotic colouring

He was very tall and
graceful in the way of athletes
his little girl clinging to him
arms around his neck
legs wrapped around his body

His voice was soft – conversational

He must have given her confidence
because she wriggled down
tottered around to explore the aisles
voice echoing clearly
telling him what she had found

They knew the young woman at the checkout
there was shared laughter
at the non-arrival of summer yet

Father proud that his daughter
with no prompting
remembered their friend
remembered to call out
her cheerful 'Bye'

Walking Together

Without knowing where it would lead
I said I would go anywhere with him
It was no casual or flippant line
to be easily dismissed

We have been from top to bottom
from side to side
of this huge land we call home

Planes for convenience
cars for extra freedom to explore
trains for our shared delight

We have been through the red centre
walked in tropical lushness
climbed mountains
seen whales
and roads unbending for miles

We have basked in the gracious surroundings
of Government House
when he was awarded the Order of Australia Medal
for services to Australian publishing

We have walked the dark corridors
of terror when the bastard cancer appeared
slogged relentlessly through recovery
into the sunlight again

Needle and Thread

A small crocheted wide-brimmed hat
was Mothers sewing kit
the crown held her thimble
between this and the base
a piece of soft felt to hold her needles

I remember watching her darning
holding a wooden mushroom inside a sock
keeping the fabric taut
as she wove threads to fill the gaping hole

She taught me the theory
but I never did master the art
of creating a smooth patch
mine were always bumpy
and most uncomfortable to wear

Many many years since those days
I found a mushroom like Mother's
I brought it home
but it sits with other carved wooden items
on the sideboard
not in my sewing box
for I know I won't use it

I pause to look at it now and then
and remember…

Fred and Ginger

He was elegance itself
perfectly poised
so light on his feet
as he leapt from table to table
or twirled a hat stand
never missing a beat
renowned for long dance sequences
caught on film with one take

Some feminists have been scathing
that Ginger did everything Fred did only
backwards wearing a flowing frock
and high-heeled shoes
and who can argue with that

They had a magic spark
whether real or imaginary
not remembered as screen lovebirds
but for their brilliance dancing together

Fish and Chips

Simple fare but exciting much competition
where in the world
have we eaten the best fish and chips?

The wharf in Hobart
served in a cone of paper
dripping with vinegar
to the sound of masts clanking
in the wind
overshadowed by kunanyi
a culinary and spiritual experience…

We stepped off the *Hogwarts Express*
at Mallaig in Scotland
and sat on the dock
watching fishing boats and ferries come and go
and feasted with much pleasure
but I might have been influenced
by the magic of riding on the train or
the gift of a Harry Potter wand
tucked safely in my bag for a grandson

How Brave the Young

A promise of summer heat
tempered by a gentle breeze
we walked along a jetty
in the afternoon sun
eating ice creams
watching a young lad daring himself
to jump off
needing his mates to assure him
the water they were wading and swimming in
was deep enough

How brave and stupid these young men are
celebrating the end of school year
weeks ahead of fun
yet risking a broken neck
a lifetime in a wheelchair
to prove they are manly

Ever was it thus

Bob and Stephen

I've watched in fascination how Stephen
has succumbed to the charms
of Bob the wattlebird

Bob flirts like a tart
(perhaps it's a Mrs Bob)
calling from a nearby tree
summoning breakfast

Bob knows we grow the native bushes
especially for him
he entertains us by hanging upside down
supping on flowers

His idea of a bath is much like a small boy's
all splash and splutter
and to our eyes
not much actual washing going on

But the Bobs brings their babies
into our garden
knowing we are watching
they show them how to lick the mango stones
and that makes us feel privileged

Not Just Coffee and Cake

We gave ourselves a treat of
smooth and creamy lattes
with lime cheesecake for Stephen
almond something for me

We looked very genteel as we sat
in a sheltered corner out of the wind
as spring-fresh leaves danced on nearby trees

Three young men sat at the next table
clearly it was time for a break from work
they looked like bright parrots
in their orange hi-vis jackets

They had big rough tough fare
no-frills flat white coffee with sugar
and very large sausage rolls
with slightly glazed pastry

They might have looked like typical Aussies
but not for them talk about footie or cricket
they were telling one of their number
about a small town in the hills
with a strong German heritage
but conceded in a considerate fashion
if he was from Germany
he might not be interested in a replica
of what he had left behind

Old and New

I learned to touch-type at high school
using an old Olivetti machine
with a detachable shield
so we couldn't see the keys

We learned to find the home keys
then endless frf ftf fgf fvf et cetera
moving around the keyboard
to the strains of 'Wheels Cha Cha'*

What a clackety-clatter filled the room
as twenty girls tried to type up
their dodgy Pitman's shorthand notes

In the last weeks of term an electric typewriter appeared
what a shock – so different to use –
hold a key down for a moment too long
and you had a row of sssssssss on the page
but we were all impatient to be able to use it

I wonder if anyone these days
learns to type as I did

Young children know their way around a keyboard
they have taken to it so easily along with
how to use the remote control or their devices

I sit at my computer or laptop –
a very different keyboard for each –
a retro one for the workhorse
I love the quiet clatter of the keys
but the laptop is almost silent
so dainty and elegant
needing such a light touch

It's interesting that neither
the computer or the laptop
can spell any better than that old Olivetti

* 'Wheels Cha Cha' was recorded in 1961 by the String-a-Longs.

Fear and Faith

Fear takes hold
scattering my thoughts
sending them along unlikely pathways
great stretches of imagination
fantastical and terrifying
always looking to
'Prepare for the worst – hope for the best'

I take a deep breath
the frightening notions fade into the ether
I know better than to pray for a specific answer
or a fix to a problem
but praying for strength and courage
will always result in having just what I need

Milton Keynes UK
Ingram Content Group UK Ltd.
UKHW012014070224
437360UK00014B/346

9 781761 096785